celebrating
mom

share, remember, cherish

JIM McCANN, FOUNDER

celebrati ns.com   **1·800 flowers**.com

**Andrews McMeel
Publishing, LLC**

Kansas City • Sydney • London

For information, write Andrews McMeel Publishing, LLC, an Andrews McMeel Universal company,
1130 Walnut Street, Kansas City, Missouri 64106

ISBN-13: 978-0-7407-9659-3
ISBN-10: 0-7407-9659-3

Library of Congress Control Number: 2009938770

10 11 12 13 14 SMA 10 9 8 7 6 5 4 3 2 1

www.andrewsmcmeel.com

ATTENTION: SCHOOLS AND BUSINESSES

Andrews McMeel books are available at quantity discounts with bulk purchase for educational, business,
or sales promotional use. For information, please write to: Special Sales Department, Andrews McMeel
Publishing, LLC, 1130 Walnut Street, Kansas City, Missouri 64106.

Project Manager: Heidi Tyline King

Designed by Alexis Siroc
Produced by SMALLWOOD & STEWART, NEW YORK CITY

Illustration credit information on page 80.

For mothers everywhere . . .

And a special thanks to our 1-800-FLOWERS.com® customers.
When we asked you to submit remembrances about your mothers on our
Web site, we had no idea that we would be showered with so many
rich stories. Too precious to keep to ourselves, your priceless memories,
both attributed and anonymous, are the inspiration for this book.

dedicated to:

....

....

....

Introduction

*I*t was my mother, Claire McCann, who taught me about compassion, the value of a hard day's work, and the importance of laughter. The lady loved to laugh. Indeed, Mom's sense of humor was so contagious that while our friends hurried outside after dinner to play, my four siblings and I would linger at the table just to hear her tell another funny story.

But of all the lessons Mom taught us, I believe the most important was her tremendous sense of family. My mother, who was raised by a single mother without aunts, uncles, or cousins living nearby, said her greatest accomplishment was her family. Money may have been tight, but she and Dad made sure that there was plenty of love to go around. And even though she is no longer with us, her love continues because of the unique sense of family she instilled in us. You see, my brother Kevin, the middle child and centerpiece of our family, was born developmentally disabled, and my siblings and I are all very active in his life and care—that's one of the reasons we have all remained in the New York area. I like to think that Mom would be proud of how we all feel responsible for his well-being—not out of guilt, but out of love.

My mom was special, but I've come to realize through the stories shared by you, our Celebrations.com and 1-800-FLOWERS.com® customers, that motherhood itself is unique. There's nothing like the love and guidance of a mom. It may appear that our business at 1-800-FLOWERS.com® is about flowers and gifts, but it's really about relationships. *Celebrating Mom* is just another way to help you express, connect, and celebrate the special times and special people in your life.

ONE

Everyday Hero

In this life we cannot do great things. We can only do small things with great love.

—MOTHER TERESA

My mother has quietly planted a garden for forty-six years. Tomatoes, potatoes, carrots, beets, cucumbers, watermelon, and radishes flourish under her tender care. When harvest arrives, she alone picks all the fruits and vegetables, giving

away basketsful to neighbors and friends. She also cans the fruits of her labors and distributes them to the elderly in our community who can no longer tend their own gardens. In doing so, she delivers more than produce— her bountiful gifts plant seeds of hope and love to all those who are blessed through her nurturing handiwork. —CHERYL M.

My mother has always had that "I'm gonna do it" attitude, but last year,

she suffered a stroke. Even though she lost 95 percent of her sight,

she continues to make blankets for her family and to do chores around

the house, such as mowing the lawn. It might take her longer than before

but she has never backed down from a challenge. —DAWN F.

♥ ♥ ♥

Mom was right. The older I get the smarter my mother becomes.

—MICHELLE P.

My mother's gift of humor

has taught me how important laughter is in life.
Whenever my dad came up with one of his crazy ideas,
she would just look at him, then mutter a dry but
hilarious comment under her breath. Mom's wit was
contagious; my brother and I are both part-time
comedians. Now, when people ask if she is proud of us,
she stares at them and says, "I'm thrilled.
It's what I dreamed of, having my children stand up on
a stage talking about my parenting. Everybody
should be so lucky. Now if only my bank clerk
will stand up and tell everyone about my finances,
my life will be complete."

A mother is a mother still,
The holiest thing alive.

—SAMUEL TAYLOR COLERIDGE

⚘ ⚘ ⚘

While there have always been feasts to celebrate mothers, the first modern observance of **Mother's Day** in the United States was in 1907. Philadelphian Anna Jarvis had sworn on her mother's grave that she would dedicate her life to establishing an official day to honor mothers both living and dead. Jarvis eventually gave up her job to undertake a full-time letter writing campaign to politicians, clergy members, business leaders, and women's clubs to persuade them in joining her efforts to lobby Congress. In 1914, Congress responded by designating the second Sunday of May as Mother's Day.

On a family vacation to a dude ranch, my husband and I were talking with excitement about our first horseback ride on one of the trails. My eighty-year-old mother piped up and said, "I believe I'd like to try that." The next thing you know, a cowboy was hoisting her onto a white horse. As she disappeared down the path with a huge smile on her face, I realized that my mom was the perfect example that you are never too old to try something new. We didn't have a camera, but the memory remains as vivid as any snapshot.

ⓥ ⓥ ⓥ

Mom taught me that serving my family is an honor, not a duty, and it's so true. When I serve my family with joy, I've always received joy from doing so. —DONNA T.

Mom always said that the pathway of motherhood is paved with self-doubt. The trick is to keep your children from knowing when you are unsure! —SHERYL P.

I came to America fifteen years ago so that my son might have a better future. That's what mothers do— always think of their children first. I learned this not by doing it for my son but from my own mother when she kissed me goodbye. —TATYANA F.

The academy... a mother's knee.

—JAMES RUSSELL LOWELL

What do girls do who haven't any mothers
to help them through their troubles?

—LOUISA MAY ALCOTT

Motherhood by the Numbers

82.8 million	Mothers in the United States in 2004
5.6 million	Stay-at-home moms in 2006
10.4 million	Single mothers living with children under 18
94.1	The number of births in Utah in 2006 per 1,000 women of childbearing age, the highest in the U.S.
52.2	The number of births in Vermont in 2006 per 1,000 women of childbearing age, the lowest in the U.S.

ⓥ   ⓥ   ⓥ

With two kids, a husband, and a full-time job, my mother went to college and got her degree. Once, I asked her why. She said, "Good, better, best. Never let it rest. Until you make your good better and your better best!" —CHRISTINA G.

When my stepmom was dying of cancer, she was in

the hospital on a respirator. One day when we were playing

soft music to soothe her, she removed her respirator

and got out of bed. Standing up, she said, "Life is short.

Don't ever be too tired to laugh, love, and dance."

And then, wearing her hospital gown and nothing on

her bare feet, she danced. —ILEANA A.

A pastor once told me, "An ounce of mother is worth a pound of clergy." —AL D.

ⓥ ⓥ ⓥ

The God to whom little boys say their prayers has a face very like their mother's. —JAMES BARRIE

ⓥ ⓥ ⓥ

According to Mom, there are
three ways to get something done:
Do it yourself,
hire someone, or forbid
your kids to do it!

—LORI F.

Being a mother is the hardest of all jobs. With kids of my own,
I know that now. I'm just thankful my own mother never gave
her two weeks' notice! —COURTNEY T.

♥ ♥ ♥

"MOM" upsidedown is "WOW!"
Mom is my "WOW" Mom, teaching me daily
to have strength, courage, patience, forgiveness, love,
and above all, faith for myself. —DEENA S.

♥ ♥ ♥

Mom taught me that when times
are tough and all else fails, beans and
macaroni really can make a meal! —GALE R.

TWO

My Greatest Fan

Youth fades; love droops;
the leaves of friendship fall;
a mother's secret hope outlives them all!

—WASHINGTON IRVING

I was sixteen years old and aching from my first broken heart. My mother sat on my bed with tears in her eyes and said, "This is the first time that I can't put a Band-Aid on your pain and make it better." —GEORGINA S.

♥ ♥ ♥

Whenever I found myself not fitting in, my mom would lecture me, "The world is full of people who want to fit a square peg into a circular hole. Don't let them knock your corners off!" —ANDREA P.

On my thirteenth birthday,
my mom gave me wonderful advice.
"Gail, darling," she said, "if you do it quickly,
quietly, and subtly, you can get away
with anything!" —GAIL W.

⌄ ⌄ ⌄

On my first day of school, I was very nervous and afraid no one would like me.
My mother looked at me with a big smile and said, "What's not to like?" —JEANNE S.

⌄ ⌄ ⌄

I will never forget my stepmother's exact words: "You are the best son
I will ever have, so remember to be a leader—not a follower. That way,
you'll know that I am always behind you." —ANGELO B.

*Whenever I fought with my mom, I went
to my grandmother for advice. She would say,*
*"No matter what has happened
today, your mother will be there for you
tomorrow."* —SARAH H.

ⓥ ⓥ ⓥ

When my mother was teaching me how to swim,
she would coax me off the edge of the pool by holding
out her hand to reassure me. To this day, when I am
afraid of something new, she will hold out her hand
and say, "Let go of the edge." —ANDREA P.

We can't all be stars,
but we can all shine. —REBECCA S.

♥ ♥ ♥

With my mother, it was never a question of whether we would go to college, but which one and what degree. Because of her work ethic and passion for learning, I'm proud to say that all four of her children have completed at least a bachelor's degree. I've completed my MBA and my brother is currently working on his. If that wasn't enough, after putting four children through school, my mom went back and earned her bachelor's degree. She made the American Dream a reality for herself and planted the seeds so her children, too, could have a better future.

The mother loves her child most divinely,
not when she surrounds him with comfort and
anticipates his wants, but when she resolutely
holds him to the highest standards and is content
with nothing less than his best.

—HAMILTON WRIGHT MABIE

When I joined the military, my mother told me, "Always remember
that what you are doing now will be one of your greatest
accomplishments. No matter what you do later in life, you will be
my hero for risking your life for me." —KACIE E.

🍃 🍃 🍃

When all of my girlfriends had boyfriends,
my mother assured me that "boys are afraid to ask out
the prettiest girls." —CORRINE G.

🍃 🍃 🍃

Many of the sweaters worn by
Mr. Rogers on the television show
Mr. Rogers Neighborhood,
were knitted by his mother.

Whenever I was concerned about being adopted,
Mom always told me that she chose me to adopt when
I was a child. She chose me. —AMANDA T.

ⓥ ⓥ ⓥ

Scientific research has found that mothers are more naturally
aroused by their infants' signals and cries than are fathers, and
they respond more readily.

ⓥ ⓥ ⓥ

Remember that you are my baby
and, therefore, better than anyone else.
But also remember that when dealing with another,
they are someone's baby, too. —JAMES C.

Whenever I asked how much she loved me, Mom would say, "You'll never find anyone who loves you as much as your mom, but I sure hope you'll give it a try!" —ANDREA P.

♥ ♥ ♥

There is only one pretty child in the world
and every mother has it.

—CHINESE PROVERB

♥ ♥ ♥

My mother loved to play with us.
We were her most important job.

—CARRIE G.

Mom always said, "There is no success with laziness!" She kept me on my toes and made me focus on my goals. Because of her, I live by these words—without a thought of ever giving up! —AISHA G.

ⓥ ⓥ ⓥ

What your children think of you is more important than what the neighbors think of you. —CHERYL W.

THREE

Unconditional Love

Motherhood:

All love begins and ends there.

—ROBERT BROWNING

Romantic love and unconditional love are experienced in different areas of the brain, according to neurophysiologists. This cognitive difference, which defines the two as completely separate feelings, is actually visible on an MRI X-ray.

♥ ♥ ♥

When I was nine years old, I remember a homeless woman approaching my mother for help. My mom, who didn't have any cash to give, took off her shoes and coat and handed them to the woman. She told me later, "I may not have much, but I will always give to someone who has less than me." To this day, if a neighbor needs a shoulder to cry on, if a stranger needs a bed to sleep in, the door to my mother's house is always open—just come on in!

Our house was the gathering spot for all the neighborhood kids. Kool-Aid stands, sleepovers, and homemade chocolate chip cookies were standard at our house. Mom had a soft spot in her heart for any under-dog, and she would encourage my five siblings and me to reach out to any child who wasn't included. That's why it has been so hard watching this loving, vibrant woman retreat deeper into herself as her Alzheimer's worsens. One night, I stayed over to help out, and Mom found me shivering under a thin blanket. When she returned with a large towel to cover me, I realized that even with her disease she was still the same nurturing, fun-loving Mom who would do whatever it took to care for someone else.

Mom always said, "Open
your heart and your home
and you will always have someone to love." —ROBIN C.

ⓥ ⓥ ⓥ

Every mother is like Moses.
She does not enter the Promised Land.
She prepares a world she will not see.

—POPE PAUL VI

ⓥ ⓥ ⓥ

When my son was born, I was so afraid I would do something wrong. My mother just looked me in the eyes and said, "If you love him with all your heart, you will never be wrong." —KELI K.

*Never give anyone less than God has given to you. That's why
mothers always have unconditional love for their children.*

—RASHONDA W.

*I was adopted when I was three months old. I am African, Irish, and
Dutch. My parents are Italian and Irish. It's no wonder Mother always
told me, "God created us in all shapes, sizes, and colors. Being different
is his definition of beauty. We are all beautiful." —*CARA S.

Everybody you love can be part of your family.

—CHERYL W.

When my dear mother was still living, she would always
say, "A family is a little world created by love." —CAROL G.

Mother always had a way of looking at others without
judgment, and she wanted me to do the same. She'd say,

"People are like crayons.

They come in different colors.

Some are brighter than others.

Some are sharp.

Some are dull.

Yet just imagine how colorful and beautiful

Life could be if they worked together.

Without all those differences,

Why, life would be just plain boring!"

—ZOYA T.

When I was getting ready to leave for college, my mother came to my
room and told me, "No matter how alone you might feel, there is always
one person who loves you unconditionally." —DAN M.

*When
my mother was about
to pass away, she comforted me
by saying, "My love will be
surrounding you forever."
Today, I know that even though she
has moved on to another world, her
love for me has not. Even now, it
surrounds me still.*

—LAURA C.

My mom knows a thing or two about unconditional love. After all, she has fostered 170 babies. That's a lot of diapers! —LORI B.

Mother is always there

. . . when lunch is forgotten,

when library books are due,

when shoes are missing,

when the tape is gone,

She finds the glue.

My favorite shirt is clean

And there's no hole in the sleeve.

She is my mother—

The best—

I do believe.

—BRIAN G.

To stepmoms around the world who accept their stepchildren as their own: I'm so glad you never read Cinderella! —BARB Y.

ⓥ ⓥ ⓥ

Do what you love and money will follow.
Follow money and you will lose what you love. —MICHAEL M.

ⓥ ⓥ ⓥ

When my mother was terminally ill, I was at her side,
her constant caregiver. Just before she passed away,
she gave me one last bit of advice: Don't be so busy
being a caregiver that you forget to just
love someone. —PAMELA M.

FOUR

Motherly Advice

The hand that rocks the cradle

is the hand that rules the world.

—WILLIAM ROSS WALLACE

I am the sixth child in a family of eleven — the true middle child. Growing up on a farm in Minnesota, my siblings and I would often complain about chores. My mother, unfazed, would simply tell us, "Just think how lucky you are. You will never have to go to prison or go on a diet, because hard work keeps you honest and slim." —JONI D.

ⱽ ⱽ ⱽ

After my father died, I was so sad for my mother. One evening while sitting at the beach watching the waves roll in to shore, I asked her how they stayed so happy. She grabbed two handfuls of sand. One she held carefully. The other she squeezed so tight the grains of sand sifted right through her fingers. I never forgot that lesson. —JOAN F.

Learn to appreciate the small
things in life. It's the smallest things that
have the biggest meanings. —RENEE B.

ⓥ ⓥ ⓥ

It is easier to build a boy than to mend a man.

—YAMELL V.

*Children are God's way of telling you your house
is way too clean!*

⊙ ⊙ ⊙

Not all hits are home runs. Sometimes you
have to take it one base at a time.
It's the same in life. Enjoy the time you spend
at each base. You will get to home plate
soon enough. —CONNIE S.

⊙ ⊙ ⊙

Whenever you are mad, write it all down in a letter—
every last hurt feeling or word. But don't send the
letter—tear it up. —AVA C.

No amount of study can prepare you
for everything in life. You have to go outside and
get dirty to learn the rest. —ANDREA P.

"You may not like what I have to say, but you
have to listen. I may not like what you have
to say, but I have to listen." This kept our line
of communication open through the years.
She always listened. Still does. —ROSE H.

Friends and family are like a life vest on a sinking ship. —DIANE V.

ⓥ ⓥ ⓥ

Mistakes happen and everyone has regrets,
but you can miss the road to the future if your eyes never leave
the rearview mirror of the past. —RENEE C.

ⓥ ⓥ ⓥ

When you look both ways
to cross the street, it wouldn't hurt to look up
and down, too! —ANDREA P.

Know when to remember and when to forget.
Know when to keep trying and when to give up.
Know when to say, "I'm sorry," and when to forgive.
—SARAH H.

⊛ ⊛ ⊛

"There will be plenty of time for that when
you're old enough…" My mom's wisdom
saved me from growing up too fast and made
me enjoy each moment. —CAROLYN I.

⊛ ⊛ ⊛

Plan ahead. Make goals. But don't be inflexible.
To be inflexible may cause you to miss the "little
extras" God wants to give you. —LINDA B.

my heavy-metal, loving mom has always looked at the bright side of life, no matter how dark the clouds on the horizon, and teaching me to do the same has been her greatest gift. When Hurricane Katrina hit, instead of feeling sorry for herself amid so much devastation and turmoil, she simply said, "At least I don't have to till my garden this year!"

♥ ♥ ♥

The more you talk, the less you hear. —MICHELLE P.

♥ ♥ ♥

Say what you mean but don't say it mean. —JOANN M.

My mother has never met a stray animal she didn't embrace. From turtles to squirrels to kittens she has **opened her home** to and lavished her **love and affection** on a motley assortment of critters. By doing so, she has taught me some of 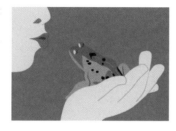 the greatest lessons of my life: Be loyal to family and friends, no matter what. **Always** greet family and friends with a smile and hug—nothing is more heartwarming than **giving and receiving love.** And the feeling of wind in your face is pure ecstasy, meaning that it's important to take time to play and enjoy the thrill of adventure. I guess you could say that everything Mom knows about love she learned from animals.

ⓥ ⓥ ⓥ

Love and be good to others, but do not forget to love and be good to yourself. —LISA S.

My mom taught me a great lesson in communication
by simply "bouncing the ball back." What she meant was that
when talking with someone, don't just agree with them.
Keep the ball in their court. —LOU H.

⊙ ⊙ ⊙

Do a job big or small, but
Do it right or not at all.

—CYNTHIA A.

⊙ ⊙ ⊙

When I was eleven, I asked my mother, "Why?" Her response?
"Don't live your life wondering why. Try to mold your path so that
you never have to ask yourself that again. That's the way you will
ultimately achieve happiness." —ISABEL R.

Manners can take you around the world. —KAREN L.

ⓥ ⓥ ⓥ

Forgiveness is

the shortest distance

between

two lives.

—JOAN L.

If you pretend to be someone you are not, you will never get to know the real person inside. —ANDREA P.

M*arry your best friend. Don't marry for lust,*
marry for friendship. It is common likes, wishes, and dreams
that will carry you through the hard times. —KIM T.

♥ ♥ ♥

Never make someone a priority when to
them you are only an option. Those who
see you as a priority are the ones who will
be there in your time of need. —JESSICA K.

♥ ♥ ♥

Let gratitude be your attitude. —KATE E.

I am not the First National Bank of Mom
and when you get old enough,
you'll know what I'm talking about. —CHRIS R.

ⓥ ⓥ ⓥ

**Get an education.
People can take away everything
from you but they can't take away
what is in your brain.** —SHAMIK P.

ⓥ ⓥ ⓥ

My mom instilled in me the importance of taking great pleasure in life's
smallest treasures: the taste of fresh coffee, the juiciness of watermelon,
a child's laugh. These precious moments are what make our lives so
fulfilling and memorable. —LAUREN K.

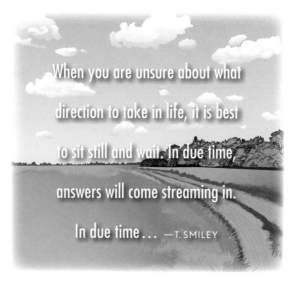

When you are unsure about what direction to take in life, it is best to sit still and wait. In due time, answers will come streaming in. In due time... —T. SMILEY

ⓥ ⓥ ⓥ

Never burn a bridge. You might be surprised at how many times you have to cross the same river! —KIMBERLY H.

If you don't leave this earth a better place than when you entered, you have no right to be here in the first place. My mom said this to me when I was growing up and it has made me love life, my family, neighbors, and myself completely. —STACIE N.

♡ ♡ ♡

What is written
on a child's heart
cannot be erased.
Choose your markings
carefully. —LORI F.

The hardest job is being a full-time mother,
but it offers the best salary—pure love. —JENNIFER H.

🌸 🌸 🌸

You can eat an elephant, but only one bite at a time. —SIMON P.

🌸 🌸 🌸

My mother has always said that having children
teaches you that patience is a virtual reality! —JAN W.

*I remember asking my mother,
"How will I know when
I'm in love?" She replied,
"You won't need to ask!"* —LINDA S.

♥ ♥ ♥

When I came home crying with a broken heart, Mom had only

one thing to say: Before someone can love you at your best,

they have to love you at your worst! —JENNIFER Y.

♥ ♥ ♥

*If you treat your family like royalty,
they will make you their queen.* —JEANETTE F.

It's not the price or size but the heart that counts.

—BONITA D.

♡ ♡ ♡

When I was younger, my mom taught me, "If you are looking for a helping hand, look at the end of your arm!" It irritated me then, but now I understand that I should always depend on myself first instead of expecting someone else to get the job done. —KIRA A.

Give God your worries.
He's going to be up all night anyway. —MARY ELLEN K.

♈ ♈ ♈

When I was small, I would overreact whenever I was cut or scraped.
Mom was no sympathizer. She'd simply say, "Oh, it's too far away
from your heart to kill you!" —AMY B.

♈ ♈ ♈

The world is your oyster.
All you have to do is crack the shell! —LISA L.

♈ ♈ ♈

The grass may be greener on the other side, but it still
has to be mowed! —LOUANNA A.

FIVE

Love Is an Action Word

*How you love your children
today is how they will
love you back tomorrow.*

—KARLINE E.

When I was nine, my mother whisked me away in the middle of the night to escape Vietnam. We left without food and lived seven months in the open air without shelter, plagued by mosquitoes and heat. When an infection left me unable to walk, my mother carried me for days on her back. Her giving didn't stop when we finally reached America. She worked in a factory and sent money to her family back home. She taught me the true meaning of love, kindness, and compassion. —CONSTANCE T.

A little girl, asked
where her home was, replied,
"Where mother is…" —KEITH B.

⚥ ⚥ ⚥

A family is not made of paper and glue,

and it's not always made of blood.

Instead, it's made with more precious

things, and it's held together with LOVE.

—LORI F.

"Do unto others . . ." is something that comes naturally to my mom. Unselfish and giving, she is always willing to sacrifice to help someone else. She makes baby blankets to donate to the hospital. She never sits down to rest . . . always on her way to take care of the next person. She will even give away a present she loves if she thinks it will put a smile on someone else's face. —SARAH B.

⚜ ⚜ ⚜

Mama always used to say, "Treat everyone as if they have a broken heart. You never know what a person might be going through." —AUDRAN S.

When I think of
Mom, I think of all her
culinary achievements. . . making
homemade cookies to serve my elemen-
tary school class, her French toast
fondue on Saturday mornings, care
packages at college with her one-of-a-kind
decorated sugar cookies. . . It was obvious
that over the years, Mom was nourishing
my body with her gourmet creations,
but now I realize she was also
nourishing my soul.

A new mom will change 7,300 diapers by her baby's second birthday and spend two minutes and five seconds each time. That adds up to six forty-hour workweeks over the two-year period.

When I was little, Mom would let us children use her good china for our tea parties. She died at thirty-eight. She knew, even then, that china is replaceable; time is not. —KAREN F.

I don't remember my mother's having any profound words of wisdom about life or growing up. She just loved us so much that it showed through her silence.

—MARIANN T.

ⓥ ⓥ ⓥ

My mother would bend over backwards to help someone, even if it was a stranger. I'll never forget the time we were grocery shopping and she saw an elderly woman struggling with her grocery cart. As she was scurrying over to help, she didn't think twice about tossing me the car keys and handing over our groceries. Scurrying by, she said, "Do you mind putting these in the car for me? I'll be right back...!" —JENNIFER T.

Whenever I grumbled about
not being able to do
something, Mom always said,
"'Can't' died seven days ago.
You can be or do anything
you set your mind to!" —DARLA B.

*Share kind words publicly but
do good works anonymously.* —CHRIS G.

Live your love! When you do, you use the strongest and most magical force in the universe! Through love, you can help children grow strong and wise, heal wounds, comfort the sick, feed the poor. Love has the power to change ugliness into beauty! —MARGOT L.

ⓥ ⓥ ⓥ

Everyone says that it takes a strong person to forgive. My mother, however, has always said it takes an even stronger person to ask forgiveness. —MARTHA B.

Time is wasted, but not affection. —ANDREA P.

⊙ ⊙ ⊙

When my mother was young, her mother gave her a ring. When I came along, she saved it to give to me. She loved that ring, but said, "I want to see you enjoy wearing it." That's love. —LINDA S.

⊙ ⊙ ⊙

For surprise notes in brown-bag lunches. For coming to ball games and recitals. For sewing. For late-night talks. For soothing a broken heart. Mom has taught me the single most valuable lesson of all: that I am loved. —CLAIRISSA C.

Watch your thoughts, for they become words.

Choose your words, for they become actions.

Understand your actions, for they become habits.

Study your habits, for they become character.

Develop your character, for it becomes your destiny.

[Although it is] scientifically unexplainable, doctors increasingly believe that mothers have a sixth sense: intuition. "Knowing without knowing how they know," moms are hotwired with an innate ability to sense and forecast when something isn't right with their young. As real as the senses of smell, taste, sight, hearing, and touch, Mom's intuition can kick in when there is no tangible reason. It seems that there is something to dear old Mom's explanation of, "I just had a feeling" after all…

♀ ♀ ♀

When asked, "What do you think is important in life?"
My mother replied:
"Time alone,
Time with friends, and
Time with God
After it all ends."
—ANDREA P.

♥ ♥ ♥

SIX

My Mother, My Friend

You aren't here merely to be sheltered under the wings of your guardian angel. You are to fly along beside her.

—CATHERINE G.

In almost every language, the word *mother* begins with **m**:

Albanian–**Mëmë; Nënë; Burim; Kryemurgeshë**

Belarusan–**Matka** Dutch–**Moeder; Moer**

English–**Mom, Mummy, Mother** Estonian–**Ema**

French–**Mere** Frisian–**Emo, Emä, Kantaäiti, Äiti**

German–**Mutter** Greek–**Màna** Hawaiian–**Makuahine**

Hindi–**Maji** Hungarian–**Anya, Fu** Italian–**Madre**

Portuguese–**Mãe** Serbian–**Majka**

Spanish–**Madre** Urdu–**Ammee**

You do not measure a productive life by your
own achievements, but by those that you make
possible for your children.

♥ ♥ ♥

When I was a girl
I never wanted to be you.
Now that I am a mom,
I pray that I can.

—DONNA M.

Be a good mother—
by any means necessary. —LINCHERRIA B.

♥ ♥ ♥

Every time I look into my ten-year-old's eyes, I see a boy filled with

love, joy, curiosity, humor, and appreciation.

He holds my hand, kisses me goodbye each morning when I drop

him off at school, and tells me he loves me every day. But even though

my son is the one doing these things, I know that

without my mother in my life and the lessons she

taught me, I wouldn't have the relationship I do

with my son. That's the greatest gift she could ever

give to me.

I came home from school one day with a juicy bit of gossip. After I told Mom, she said, "Believe half of what you see and none of what you hear." That bit of advice has rung true so many times in my life. —APRIL F.

♥ ♥ ♥

I know without a doubt that even though I am adopted, I was born to be my mother's daughter. She is the first person I call when I'm sad, when I'm happy, or when I'm bored. She has taught me the values of strength, independence, honesty, and love. She is my lifeline, my support, my rock. She is more than my mother; she is my friend.

Just when you thought life didn't get more
beautiful and precious than giving birth to your
own daughter, you are in the delivery room
with your daughter as she gives birth to hers.

—JOANNA V.

⊙ ⊙ ⊙

Make plans for some one-on-one time, whether it's just a manicure,

lunch, or shopping. When I was nineteen, my mother developed MS and

I never had the chance to share moments like these with her as an

adult. I miss that. Now that I'm a mom with grown children, I want to

make sure they have a chance to experience these seemingly ordinary

but precious times together. —JANET T.

Mom, remember those ugly brown

corduroy pants I wore? And that salty green dough—

not the store-bought Play-Doh? Now that I am

grown—and the seventies are over—I am thankful

for clean clothes, homemade dough, but most of all, for

having a mom who is always there for me and

not afraid to be different! —SANDRA D.

My Mother, My Friend

A mother is the truest friend we have,

When trials heavy and sudden,

Fall upon us;

When adversity takes the place of prosperity;

When friends who rejoice with us in our sunshine

Desert us;

When trouble thickens around us,

Still she will cling to us,

And endeavor by her kind precepts and counsels

To dissipate the clouds of darkness,

And cause peace to return to our hearts.

—WASHINGTON IRVING

When my brothers and sisters and I got into arguments, my mother would sit us down and make each of us tell one joke. It was her way of teaching us her philosophy about life—that laughter is the best medicine. —SARAH H.

♥ ♥ ♥

I see the joy and beauty in motherhood because you did. Thank you. —CRYSTALIN D.

illustration credits